Francis Frith's
AROUND DORSET

PHOTOGRAPHIC MEMORIES

Francis Frith's
AROUND DORSET

◆

John Bainbridge

FRITH
BOOK Co

First published in the United Kingdom in 1999 by
Frith Book Company Ltd

Hardback Edition 1999
ISBN 1-85937-075-6

Hardback Reprinted in 2001

Paperback Edition 2001
ISBN 1-85937-269-4

Paperback Reprinted in 2002

British Library Cataloguing in Publication Data

Francis Frith's Around Dorset
John Bainbridge

Frith Book Company Ltd
Frith's Barn, Teffont,
Salisbury, Wiltshire SP3 5QP
Tel: +44 (0) 1722 716 376
Email: info@francisfrith.co.uk
www.francisfrith.co.uk

Printed and bound in Great Britain

CONTENTS

Francis Frith: Victorian Pioneer   7

Frith's Archive - A Unique Legacy   10

Dorset - An Introduction   12

The Inland Towns   13

The Rural Heartland   42

Along the Coast   72

Index   117

Free Mounted Print Voucher   121

FRANCIS FRITH: *Victorian Pioneer*

FRANCIS FRITH, Victorian founder of the world-famous photographic archive, was a complex and multitudinous man. A devout Quaker and a highly successful Victorian businessman, he was both philosophic by nature and pioneering in outlook.

By 1855 Francis Frith had already established a wholesale grocery business in Liverpool, and sold it for the astonishing sum of £200,000, which is the equivalent today of over £15,000,000. Now a multi-millionaire, he was able to indulge his passion for travel. As a child he had pored over travel books written by early explorers, and his fancy and imagination had been stirred by family holidays to the sublime mountain regions of Wales and Scotland. 'What a land of spirit-stirring and enriching scenes and places!' he had written. He was to return to these scenes of grandeur in later years to 'recapture the thousands of vivid and tender memories', but with a different purpose. Now in his thirties, and captivated by the new science of photography, Frith set out on a series of pioneering journeys to the Nile regions that occupied him from 1856 until 1860.

INTRIGUE AND ADVENTURE

He took with him on his travels a specially-designed wicker carriage that acted as both dark-room and sleeping chamber. These far-flung journeys were packed with intrigue and adventure. In his life story, written when he was sixty-three, Frith tells of being held captive by bandits, and of fighting 'an awful midnight battle to the very point of surrender with a deadly pack of hungry, wild dogs'. Sporting flowing Arab costume, Frith arrived at Akaba by camel seventy years before Lawrence, where he encountered 'desert princes and rival sheikhs, blazing with jewel-hilted swords'.

During these extraordinary adventures he was assiduously exploring the desert regions bordering the Nile and patiently recording the antiquities and peoples with his camera. He was the first photographer to venture beyond the sixth cataract. Africa was still the mysterious 'Dark Continent', and Stanley and Livingstone's historic meeting was a decade into the future. The conditions for picture taking confound belief. He laboured for hours in his wicker dark-room in the sweltering heat of the desert, while the volatile chemicals fizzed dangerously in their trays. Often he was forced to work in remote tombs and caves

where conditions were cooler. Back in London he exhibited his photographs and was 'rapturously cheered' by members of the Royal Society. His reputation as a photographer was made overnight. An eminent modern historian has likened their impact on the population of the time to that on our own generation of the first photographs taken on the surface of the moon.

VENTURE OF A LIFE-TIME

Characteristically, Frith quickly spotted the opportunity to create a new business as a specialist publisher of photographs. He lived in an era of immense and sometimes violent change. For the poor in the early part of Victoria's reign work was a drudge and the hours long, and people had precious little free time to enjoy themselves.

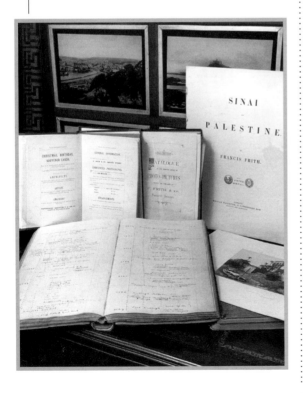

Most had no transport other than a cart or gig at their disposal, and had not travelled far beyond the boundaries of their own town or village. However, by the 1870s, the railways had threaded their way across the country, and Bank Holidays and half-day Saturdays had been made obligatory by Act of Parliament. All of a sudden the ordinary working man and his family were able to enjoy days out and see a little more of the world.

With characteristic business acumen, Francis Frith foresaw that these new tourists would enjoy having souvenirs to commemorate their days out. In 1860 he married Mary Ann Rosling and set out with the intention of photographing every city, town and village in Britain. For the next thirty years he travelled the country by train and by pony and trap, producing fine photographs of seaside resorts and beauty spots that were keenly bought by millions of Victorians. These prints were painstakingly pasted into family albums and pored over during the dark nights of winter, rekindling precious memories of summer excursions.

THE RISE OF FRITH & CO

Frith's studio was soon supplying retail shops all over the country. To meet the demand he gathered about him a small team of photographers, and published the work of independent artist-photographers of the calibre of Roger Fenton and Francis Bedford. In order to gain some understanding of the scale of Frith's business one only has to look at the catalogue issued by Frith & Co in 1886: it runs to some 670

pages, listing not only many thousands of views of the British Isles but also many photographs of most European countries, and China, Japan, the USA and Canada – note the sample page shown above from the hand-written *Frith & Co* ledgers detailing pictures taken. By 1890 Frith had created the greatest specialist photographic publishing company in the world, with over 2,000 outlets – more than the combined number that Boots and WH Smith have today! The picture on the right shows the *Frith & Co* display board at Ingleton in the Yorkshire Dales. Beautifully constructed with mahogany frame and gilt inserts, it could display up to a dozen local scenes.

POSTCARD BONANZA

The ever-popular holiday postcard we know today took many years to develop. In 1870 the Post Office issued the first plain cards, with a pre-printed stamp on one face. In 1894 they allowed other publishers' cards to be sent through the mail with an attached adhesive halfpenny stamp. Demand grew rapidly, and in 1895 a new size of postcard was permitted called the court card, but there was little room for illustration. In 1899, a year after Frith's death, a new card measuring 5.5 x 3.5 inches became the standard format, but it was not until 1902 that the divided back came into being, with address and message on one face and a full-size illustration on the other. *Frith & Co* were in the vanguard of postcard development, and Frith's sons Eustace and Cyril continued their father's monumental task, expanding the number of views offered to the public and recording more and more places in Britain, as the coasts and countryside were opened up to mass travel.

Francis Frith died in 1898 at his villa in Cannes, his great project still growing. The archive he created continued in business for another seventy years. By 1970 it contained over a third of a million pictures of 7,000 cities, towns and villages. The massive photographic record Frith has left to us stands as a living monument to a special and very remarkable man.

Frith's Archive: *A Unique Legacy*

FRANCIS FRITH'S legacy to us today is of immense significance and value, for the magnificent archive of evocative photographs he created provides a unique record of change in 7,000 cities, towns and villages throughout Britain over a century and more. Frith and his fellow studio photographers revisited locations many times down the years to update their views, compiling for us an enthralling and colourful pageant of British life and character.

We tend to think of Frith's sepia views of Britain as nostalgic, for most of us use them to conjure up memories of places in our own lives with which we have family associations. It often makes us forget that to Francis Frith they were records of daily life as it was actually being lived in the cities, towns and villages of his day. The Victorian age was one of great and often bewildering change for ordinary people, and though the pictures evoke an impression of slower times, life was as busy and hectic as it is today.

We are fortunate that Frith was a photographer of the people, dedicated to recording the minutiae of everyday life. For it is this sheer wealth of visual data, the painstaking chronicle of changes in dress, transport, street layouts, buildings, housing, engineering and landscape that captivates us so much today. His remarkable images offer us a powerful link with the past and with the lives of our ancestors.

TODAY'S TECHNOLOGY

Computers have now made it possible for Frith's many thousands of images to be accessed almost instantly. In the Frith archive today, each photograph is carefully 'digitised' then stored on a CD Rom. Frith archivists can locate a single photograph amongst thousands within seconds. Views can be catalogued and sorted under a variety of categories of place and content to the immediate benefit of researchers. Inexpensive reference prints can be created for them at the touch of a mouse button, and a wide range of books and other printed materials assembled and published for a wider, more general readership - in the next twelve months over a hundred Frith local history titles will be published! The

See Frith at www.francisfrith.co.uk

day-to-day workings of the archive are very different from how they were in Francis Frith's time: imagine the herculean task of sorting through eleven tons of glass negatives as Frith had to do to locate a particular sequence of pictures! Yet the archive still prides itself on maintaining the same high standards of excellence laid down by Francis Frith, including the painstaking cataloguing and indexing of every view.

It is curious to reflect on how the internet now allows researchers in America and elsewhere greater instant access to the archive than Frith himself ever enjoyed. Many thousands of individual views can be called up on screen within seconds on one of the Frith internet sites, enabling people living continents away to revisit the streets of their ancestral home town, or view places in Britain where they have enjoyed holidays. Many overseas researchers welcome the chance to view special theme selections, such as transport, sports, costume and ancient monuments.

We are certain that Francis Frith would have heartily approved of these modern developments, for he himself was always working at the very limits of Victorian photographic technology.

THE VALUE OF THE ARCHIVE TODAY

Because of the benefits brought by the computer, Frith's images are increasingly studied by social historians, by researchers into genealogy and ancestory, by architects, town planners, and by teachers and schoolchildren involved in local history projects. In addition, the archive offers every one of us a unique opportunity to examine the places where we and our families have lived and worked down the years. Immensely successful in Frith's own era, the archive is now, a century and more on, entering a new phase of popularity.

THE PAST IN TUNE WITH THE FUTURE

Historians consider the Francis Frith Collection to be of prime national importance. It is the only archive of its kind remaining in private ownership and has been valued at a million pounds. However, this figure is now rapidly increasing as digital technology enables more and more people around the world to enjoy its benefits.

Francis Frith's archive is now housed in an historic timber barn in the beautiful village of Teffont in Wiltshire. Its founder would not recognize the archive office as it is today. In place of the many thousands of dusty boxes containing glass plate negatives and an all-pervading odour of photographic chemicals, there are now ranks of computer screens. He would be amazed to watch his images travelling round the world at unimaginable speeds through network and internet lines.

The archive's future is both bright and exciting. Francis Frith, with his unshakeable belief in making photographs available to the greatest number of people, would undoubtedly approve of what is being done today with his lifetime's work. His photographs, depicting our shared past, are now bringing pleasure and enlightenment to millions around the world a century and more after his death.

DORSET – *An Introduction*

Dorset is a county of contrasts, but with an identity all its own. Few visitors fail to fall under the spell of its scenic beauty, its deep historical and literary associations, and its inherent peace and tranquillity. Despite the growth in population, the intrusion of some modern industries, and a considerable increase in traffic since Frith visited, Dorset remains unspoiled and rural. Few English counties have been quite so fortunate.

From the deep valleys and woodlands of the west, where the county slips imperceptibly into Devon, to the high chalk downlands with their ancient ridge paths, where it is still possible to wander for much of the day with only sheep and farmworkers for company, to the lowland heaths where rare birds and butterflies crouch in the heather and gorse, this land is as English as anyone could imagine.

Many of the villages could have come straight from a picture on a box of biscuits: it is as though someone with the eye of an artist had made them with great care and purpose. Rarely do the constructions of man complement the hand of nature quite so well.

Dorset is bounded to the south by a long coastline of exquisite beauty and variety. To walk along the Dorset Coast Path, part of the longer South West Way, from the fossil cliffs of Lyme Regis to the vast expanse of Poole Harbour, would be an excellent introduction to Dorset for anyone unfamiliar with the district.

Pick any Dorset town and it is not hard to find traces of English history. Many of these settlements were here when this land was an outpost of the Roman Empire. Saxon kings endowed their religious buildings, and some lie buried in the churches they cherished. History is everywhere, only waiting to be discovered and interpreted.

Where change has occurred since the photographs in this book were taken, it has not been dramatic. Add a little more traffic and a few altered shop signs and the view is essentially the same. Away from the larger towns there has scarcely been any change at all, and it is possible to compare the scenes directly. All who love Dorset welcome this sense of permanency. Long may the county remain unchanged!

THE INLAND TOWNS

The wise visitor will stroll around Dorset's towns either in the first light of morning or the quiet of evening. Then, motor traffic is at its minimum, and it is possible to see the towns as the Frith photographer would have done. Only then can you appreciate the joys of their diverse architecture, their historical and literary associations and, above all, their sheer Englishness.

Most were settlements when the Romans held power, but the layout of many is pure Saxon. For this was the heartland of the old kingdom of Wessex, and towns such as Shaftesbury, Sherborne and Wareham still hold echoes of those powerful Saxon kings - Ethelred, Ethelbald, Ethelbert and Alfred - some of whom are buried in the honey-coloured stone churches, abbeys and minsters of the locality.

For fans of Thomas Hardy, Dorchester is for ever Casterbridge, capital of the Wessex of his marvellous novels. There is probably no better way of exploring its streets than with a copy of 'The Mayor of Casterbridge', follow-ing in the steps of Hardy's sad hero Michael Henchard. Such a stroll will reveal many of Dorchester's odd and delightful corners. This tour should be supplemented by a visit to the local museum, where Hardy's study has been meticulously recreated.

Bridport, Blandford and Wimborne long thrived as market towns, commercial centres for the villages and farmlands of a wider, unspoiled countryside. Each had their own industries. At Bridport, for instance, rope-making provided for the local economy when the town failed as a port. Such trades were important when alternative work, such as agri-culture and fishing, were so dependent on the vagaries of weather, supply failure and general unemployment.

All of these towns have a close relation-ship with their surrounding countryside; the fields, woods and downlands are seldom more than a half-hour's walk from their centres. To some extent, the green mantle of the Dorset countryside has shaped their development as much as the hand of man.

DORCHESTER, FROM THE RIVER FROME 1930 83388
This fine view of Dorchester from the meadows alongside the River Frome shows the county town of Dorset much as Thomas Hardy would have known it when, as an apprentice architect, he would walk there each day from his home in the neighbouring hamlet of Bockhampton.

DORCHESTER, EAST STREET 1891 28512
A long highway, for centuries a major coaching route, passes through Dorchester. Thomas Hardy would walk this way to work, often stopping along the way to talk to that other great Dorset poet William Barnes.

DORCHESTER, CORNHILL 1891 28514

A splendid variety of architecture, ranging from medieval through Georgian to Victorian, greets the visitor to Dorchester. A stroll around its streets and tree-lined walks can recapture the mood of Hardy's famous novel 'The Mayor of Casterbridge'.

DORCHESTER, THE TOWN HALL 1903 50841

Dorchester, as the name suggests, was an important settlement during the heyday of the Roman Empire, and the surrounding countryside is rich in Roman remains. Just south of the town is the amphitheatre of Maumbury Rings, which was to Dorchester 'what the Coliseum was to Rome', according to Hardy.

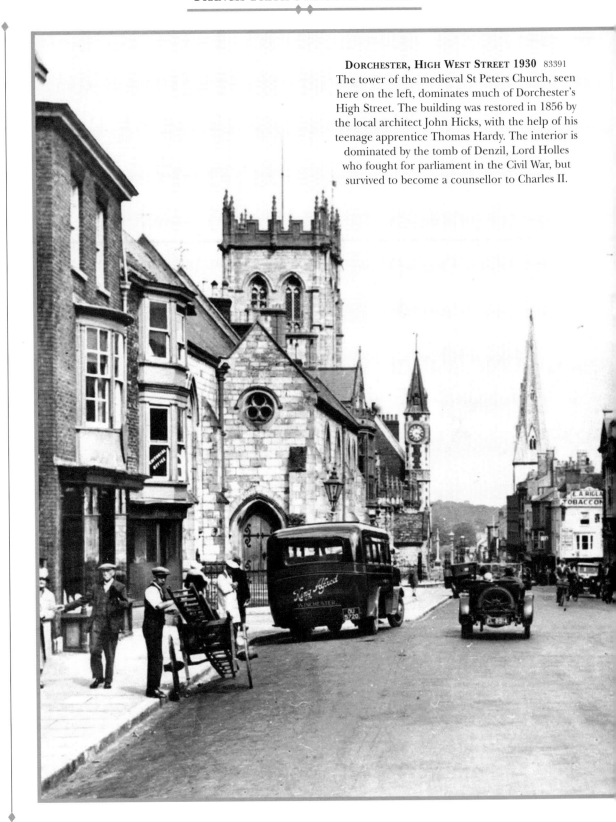

DORCHESTER, HIGH WEST STREET 1930 83391
The tower of the medieval St Peters Church, seen here on the left, dominates much of Dorchester's High Street. The building was restored in 1856 by the local architect John Hicks, with the help of his teenage apprentice Thomas Hardy. The interior is dominated by the tomb of Denzil, Lord Holles who fought for parliament in the Civil War, but survived to become a counsellor to Charles II.

DORCHESTER, THE POST OFFICE 1913 65612
Dorchester has been an important centre for communications from Roman times to the heyday of the stage coach, when the posthorn would have been heard daily on this important mail route. This fine and imposing Post Office building shows how highly regarded was the Royal Mail until well into the 20th century.

DORCHESTER, WEST STREET 1891 28515
A walk down West Street from Thomas Hardy's statue will bring the visitor to the County Museum, where the novelist's study has been faithfully recreated, complete with the pens used to write each novel.

DORCHESTER. HANGMAN'S COTTAGE 1898   41163

DORCHESTER
Hangman's Cottage 1898
Hangman's Cottage, seen here on the left, was the home of the town's resident executioner in the 19th century. The young Thomas Hardy was shocked and fascinated by the public execution of a woman in Dorchester and was unable to dispel the image from his mind, using the scene for the climax of 'Tess of the D'Urbervilles'.

◆

DORCHESTER
A Backwater 1913
Two young people pose for the camera by Dorchester's sluice gates. Only a year later thousands of young men from the county marched away to the trenches of the Great War. War memorials throughout Dorset show how many never returned. Dorchester itself lost 230 men in battle.

DORCHESTER, A BACKWATER 1913   65618X

HIGHER BOCKHAMPTON, THOMAS HARDY'S BIRTHPLACE 1930 83400
Thomas Hardy was born in this cottage in 1840 and wrote his first three novels whilst living there. He retained an interest in the family home until the end of his life. The National Trust acquired the house and surroundings in 1948, and it is regularly open to the public.

DORCHESTER, THOMAS HARDY'S HOME 1930 83402
Hardy designed Max Gate as his final home and wrote his greatest novels there. Many famous personalities, such as Lawrence of Arabia, came here to pay homage to the grand old man of English letters. The poet and novelist died here in 1928.

BRIDPORT, EAST STREET 1897 40080
Even though Dorchester is the county town, there is little doubt that Bridport is the capital of West Dorset. A thousand years ago in the reign of Edward the Confessor this important town comprised a mint, a priory and a hundred and twenty houses.

BRIDPORT, AN OLD COTTAGE 1897 40089
This delightful photograph shows that even a century ago visitors were catered for in Bridport. In those days the lemonade and ginger beer would almost certainly have been home-made. The watering cans were no doubt ready to water the plants in the cottage garden.

BRIDPORT, EAST STREET 1904 52756
The wide main streets of Bridport were originally designed to be highways, market venues and workshops. Rope and net making were considerable industries in previous centuries and the width of the thoroughfares facilitated their manufacture.

BRIDPORT, W. FROST'S SHOP FRONT 1909 61645x

BRIDPORT
W. Frost's shop front 1909
Mr Frost's printing works and shop would have been kept busy in a market town like Bridport, producing a local newspaper, bills of sale and stationery for farmers and small traders. Books and newspapers would have been on sale for those who had the leisure to read them.

◆

BRIDPORT
West Street 1930
This town was a considerable port in the middle ages, but the silting up of its ancient harbour led to a decline in trade. In later centuries, the port of West Bay was opened downstream and goods came once more by sea and into this ancient town.

BRIDPORT, WEST STREET 1930 83344

BRIDPORT, WEST STREET 1930 83342X
Bridport's Town Hall intrudes into the path of traffic and pedestrians at the junction of West and South Streets. Even as early as the 1930s the increase in motor traffic led to calls for a bypass, though it took half a century before one was constructed.

SHAFTESBURY, THE TOWN HALL c1902 S593501
The hilltop town of Shaftesbury has wide views over Blackmoor Vale and thousands of acres of rolling Dorset countryside. Some locals still use its old name of Shaston. Alfred the Great and Edmund Ironside endowed Shaftesbury with buildings and land, Edward the Martyr is buried here and King Canute died in the town.

SHAFTESBURY, THE TRIANGLE c1950 S593008

The Grosvenor Hotel, seen here on the right, houses a famous piece of Victorian furniture, the Chevy Chase Sideboard. This was carved from solid oak, representing the border battle of that name which took place in 1388.

SHAFTESBURY, SALISBURY STREET c1955 S593002

Shaftesbury had, and still has, though not to the same extent, a large number of ancient inns, catering as it did for travellers on the London Road. An unkind slur alleged that 'beer is more common in Shaftesbury than any other fluid'.

SHERBORNE, FROM THE SLOPES 1895 37076

Sherborne is, by some people's estimation, the most beautiful of the Dorset towns. It is certainly a settlement of considerable historic interest: it has connections with a number of characters from English history, including Saxon kings, Cardinal Wolsey, Sir Walter Raleigh and Oliver Cromwell.

SHERBORNE, THE ABBEY 1924 75943

Sherborne Abbey is the burial place of two Saxon kings, Ethelbald and Ethelbert, the two elder brothers of Alfred the Great. The building itself, though Saxon in origin, is mainly Norman and Perpendicular. Its warm stone gives the building an attractive feel in a town of beautiful buildings.

SHERBORNE, SOUTH STREET 1887 19670

For many years Sherborne was the capital of the Saxon kingdom of Wessex. As a cathedral town at that time its bishops were expected to be warriors as well as theologians. No less than three bishops died fighting the Danes.

SHERBORNE, CHEAP STREET 1903 49719

In Cheap Street is the Conduit, originally situated in the cloisters of Sherborne Abbey and used as a washing house, or lavatorium. The Conduit was moved to its present location after the dissolution of the religious house and used as a market building. It has since served as a police station, reading room and bank.

SHERBORNE
Old Castle Ruins 1900
Sherborne Castle was built on the site of the Saxon Bishops' Palace by the Norman warlord Roger of Caen. It has had many owners, including Sir Walter Raleigh. The castle was 'slighted' in the Civil War to make it indefensible. Its gatehouse is Norman with Tudor windows and facings.

◆

SHERBORNE
Sherborne School for Girls 1912
Sherborne is famous for its public schools, and on most days in term time pupils can be seen threading their way around the old town. The presence of the schools gives Sherborne an academic air, rather like an old university town.

SHERBORNE, OLD CASTLE RUINS 1900 46082

SHERBORNE, SHERBORNE SCHOOL FOR GIRLS 1912 64658

WAREHAM, WEST STREET 1949 W173035
The Romans originally laid out the streets of
Wareham to match the four points of the
compass. The street names of today, North,
South, East and West, match this design. Most
of the buildings seen here date from after the
great fire which destroyed Wareham in 1762.

WAREHAM, NORTH STREET 1949 W173034

Wareham lies within earthen ramparts raised for its defence by Alfred the Great in the 9th century, for this was an important Saxon borough. The church here has a fine monument to Lawrence of Arabia sculpted by Eric Kennington, though that troubled warrior is actually buried a few miles away at Moreton.

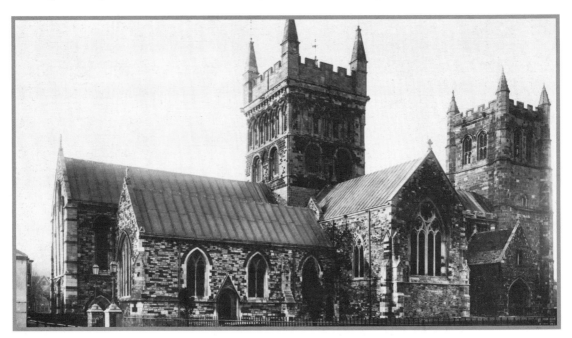

WIMBORNE, THE MINSTER 1891 29630

Wimborne Minster dominates the winding streets of the medieval town to which it gives its name. The Normans mostly created the splendid place of worship we see today, though on an earlier Saxon site. There are few finer buildings in England.

WIMBORNE
The Minster Clock 1886

This clock probably dates from the 14th century, though the works were replaced in the 18th century. The face shows the sun, moon and stars circling the earth, the sun taking twenty-four hours to complete a circuit, and the darkening moon a lunar month.

◆

WIMBORNE
The Minster Crypt 1886

There are many fine tombs within the Minster, including that of Saint Ethelred, a brother of Alfred, who was killed by the Danes in 873. John Beaufort, the grandfather of Henry VIII, lies buried nearby.

WIMBORNE, THE MINSTER CLOCK 1886   19485

WIMBORNE, THE MINSTER CRYPT 1886   19488

WIMBORNE, THE MINSTER CHAINED LIBRARY 1899 43713
The Minster's Chained Library dates back to 1686. It is one of the biggest in the country with over 200 volumes, the oldest dating back to 1343. The volume of Raleigh's 'History of the World' has a hole burnt through 104 pages, supposedly caused by the poet Matthew Prior who fell asleep with an unguarded candle nearby.

WIMBORNE, MARKET PLACE 1891 29635
Astonishingly, the Dorset topographer Sir Frederick Treves described Wimborne as a 'characterless place...successfully mediocre'. In fact, visitors threading their way around the streets can admire a splendid array of Georgian and Victorian architecture.

WIMBORNE, HIGH STREET 1904 52472

Thomas Hardy lived in Wimborne for a short period during his first marriage. The town features slightly in his novel 'Two on a Tower', which was written at that time. Hardy was fond of sitting in the Minster with only the organist and his music for company.

WIMBORNE, THE SQUARE 1904 52474

Wimborne was for centuries an important agricultural and commercial centre. This picture of the Square shows the Crown Hotel, an old coaching house, forced to offer every attraction from livery to billiards, as the road network suffered during the dominant days of the railway.

WIMBORNE, EAST STREET 1904 52475
The visitor to Wimborne today will find it
hard to imagine the streets being as empty as
this, with pedestrians and cyclists dominating
the scene. This is Wimborne as Thomas
Hardy, a keen cyclist, would have known it
thirty years earlier.

BADBURY RINGS, THE AVENUE OF TREES 1936 87209

The long avenue of beech trees which lines the road beyond Wimborne, towards the ancient hillfort of Badbury Rings, is one of the finest sights in England. In the autumn, the overhanging branches form a seemingly never-ending tunnel of gold as the traveller journeys onward.

BADBURY RINGS, THE HILLFORT 1899 43722

Situated near to the junction of two Roman roads and several prehistoric trackways, the Iron Age hillfort of Badbury Rings dominates the surrounding downland. Tradition alleges that Badbury is the site of Mount Badon, where King Arthur defeated the invading Saxons in the 6th century.

BLANDFORD FORUM
Market Place c1955

One of Blandford's ancient industries was glass painting. The 17th-century topographer Aubrey noted 'Old Harding of Blandford in Dorsetshire, where I went to schoole, was the only country glasse painter that ever I knew. Upon plaie daies I was wont to visit his shop and furnaces. He dyed about 1643, aged about 83 or more'.

◆

BLANDFORD FORUM
The Crown Hotel c1955

The Crown Hotel, situated at the west end of Blandford's market place, was refaced in its original Georgian style in 1938. Its size indicates the relative wealth of this small country town well into the 20th century - its fortunes boosted by the presence of adjacent military camps.

BLANDFORD FORUM, MARKET PLACE c1955 B282031

BLANDFORD FORUM, THE CROWN HOTEL c1955 B282019

BLANDFORD FORUM, MARKET PLACE 1950 B282003
The market place at Blandford held important sheep fairs until well into the 20th century, with the town council taking a toll on all sales. Blandford has declined as an agricultural centre, but is a popular shopping venue for the inhabitants of the surrounding villages.

THE RURAL HEARTLAND

Dorset's rural heartland is best explored on foot, for walking the lanes and paths which thread from village to village is the only way to seek out the scenes captured at a vital time in their history by the Frith photographer. Other forms of transport are too swift: the greater delights of Dorset's scenery are missed by using them. Each mile of the way, you will know that you are treading in the footsteps of Iron Age man, Roman legions, quarrymen, farmers and poets. It says a lot for this landscape that artists of all kinds have responded to it and interpreted it in diverse ways.

This rural hinterland is both beautiful and mysterious, filled with history and crammed with legend. Until the 19th century it would seldom have been visited by the outsider; its deep wooded valleys, chalk downlands and secluded heaths form a physical and mental barrier to the intruder. The locals themselves would hardly have strayed much beyond their villages, except to visit nearby market towns, or to drive livestock from parish to parish

along the ancient droving routes which can still be followed today. Only the adventurous minority - tinkers, smugglers, rebels and the gentry - would have gone further.

Life in these agricultural communities was not always a pastoral idyll. Many of the charming cottages we admire today, and which the Frith photographer captured so well, would have been rural slums a century or more ago, for the lot of the Dorset farmworker could be hard. Once, this peaceful landscape teemed with social agitation as the Swing Riots and the transportation of the Tolpuddle Martyrs brought dissent and rebellion to the village squares and green meadows of inland Dorset.

These communities must have witnessed similar upheavals throughout the centuries, lost as they are in time. Fortifications, from Iron Age hillfort to gaunt Norman castle, bear witness to earlier conflicts. But there was light as well as darkness. The churches, whose peals of bells sound sweetly over the surrounding downlands, show the peaceful energies of Saxon and Norman builders - and often the

worst excesses of Victorian 'restorers'. The residents of a hundred manor houses shaped the landscape with their ordered parklands and pheasant preserves, sometimes removing whole villages to improve a view. Every plough and woodsman's axe has marked the land in some way, for the history of all society is writ large across this countryside.

Thomas Hardy captured all of this landscape in his series of Wessex novels, at a time before their character was changed by the intrusions of modern life and the deadening influence of far-distant urban philosophies. Only a child of the Dorset heathlands, as Hardy was, could have portrayed this lovely pastoral landscape with such accuracy and affection.

ALLINGTON, THE VILLAGE 1902 48399
Allington has now been absorbed by its larger neighbour Bridport, and tends to be overlooked by visitors to that town. But it still retains something of the rural charm shown in this photograph, though its roads are seldom as quiet as this.

BEAMINSTER, 'FURGE' LANE 1907 58145

BEAMINSTER
'Furge' Lane 1907

'Sweet Be'mister, that bist a-bound By green and woody hills all round, Wi' hedges reachen up between A thousan' vields of zummer green, Where Elems' lofty heads do drow Their sheades vor hay-makers below, An wild hedge-flour's do charm the souls O' maidens in their evenin' strolls'. William Barnes.

◆

BEAMINSTER
The Village 1902

Beaminster today is not so very different from the old Dorset village that the dialect poet William Barnes would have known. Its name is always pronounced Be'mister as in Barnes' famous poem, and it remains the quaint old market town it always was.

BEAMINSTER, THE VILLAGE 1902 48422

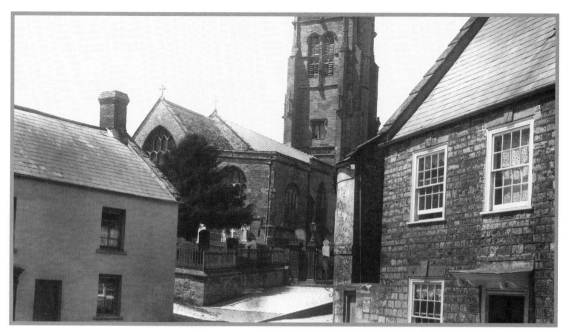

BEAMINSTER, THE CHURCH 1902 48431

Beaminster Church is mostly 15th century, though the dramatic perpendicular tower, which dominates the surrounding houses, and the arcade are 13th century. Inside are many monuments to the Strode family, who lived in nearby Parnham House.

BEAMINSTER, HOGSHILL STREET 1902 48425

In its heyday, Beaminster could boast at least seventeen inns, built to cater for the many farmers who came to town for the weekly market, as well as passengers on the Crewkerne to Bridport coach. The New Inn, shown here, was favoured by rural workers who would come to sample Mr Weaver's famous ales.

BEAMINSTER, MARKET PLACE 1907 58134

Beaminster is the 'Emminster' of Hardy's novel 'Tess of the D'Urbervilles'. Here was the home of Tess's estranged husband Angel Clare, and here Tess ended her long and fruitless walk across Dorset to meet the Clare family. Hardy drew a very accurate picture of Beaminster, and it is possible to follow in his heroine's footsteps.

BINDON ABBEY, THE GATEWAY 1894 34614

Bindon Abbey was the location of an important Cistercian monastery and dates back to 1172. Little remains of the original building; this neo-gothic gatehouse dates back only to the 1790s. It is the only part of the Abbey visible to the public.

BOVINGTON, VIEW FROM THE TANK TRAINING GROUNDS c1955 B734004

Bovington Camp dates back to the First World War, and is the home of the Royal Armoured Corps. The surrounding heathland is heavily used for tank training. It was in a hospital here that Lawrence of Arabia died following his motorcycle crash in 1935.

BOVINGTON, THE A.F.V. GARAGE c1955 B734005

Bovington is the home of the popular tank museum, where a great many tanks and armoured military vehicles can be seen. Tanks can be seen which date back from the original secret weapon of the First World War. There is also a permanent exhibition of Lawrence of Arabia memorabilia.

BRADPOLE, THE VILLAGE 1897 40093
Bradpole is another ancient West Dorset village, now overshadowed by its larger neighbour Bridport. It was the birthplace of the educational reformer W E Forster, who introduced into parliament the pioneering Education Bill of 1870 which provided a free education for all children.

CANFORD, THE MANOR C1886 19490
Canford Manor, not far from Wimborne, dates from the early years of the 19th century, though it stands on the site of an ancient house which once belonged to the Earls of Salisbury. The present building, now a public school, was for many years the country seat of Lord Wimborne.

CHARMINSTER
The Village 1913

Charminster stands across the valley of the River Frome from Dorchester. It has grown considerably since this picture was taken. The nearby manor house of Wolfeton was built in the reign of Henry VIII, and was for many years the home of the Trenchard family.

◆

CHARMINSTER
The Church 1922

The 15th-century tower of Charminster's church dominates the valley of the River Cerne, and was built under the direction of Sir Thomas Trenchard. Parts of the building date back to the 12th century. The wooden pulpit is three hundred and fifty years old.

CHARMINSTER, THE VILLAGE 1913 65630

CHARMINSTER, THE CHURCH 1922 72760

CHARMINSTER, THE VILLAGE 1922 72757

In 1506 the Archduke Phillip of Austria and his wife the Spanish Infanta Joanna were brought to Charminster after being cast ashore on the Dorset coast. Their local interpreter John Russell made such an impression on the royal couple that they took him to the court of Henry VII, where he became a leading courtier. Henry VIII awarded Russell Woburn Abbey as a reward for service, and his descendants became Dukes of Bedford.

CORFE CASTLE, THE CASTLE AND THE VILLAGE 1890 25562

The ruins of Corfe Castle dominate the parish and village to which it has given its name. The original Saxon fortification was succeeded by the extensive Norman castle seen today. The Castle held out for the king during the English Civil War, and attempts were made to 'slight' the castle afterwards. Although it was damaged, the castle resisted the massive destruction that was intended for it.

CORFE CASTLE, FROM THE CHURCH 1897 40318

CORFE CASTLE
From the Church 1897

One of the darkest deeds in English history took place in Saxon times, when King Edward was murdered by his stepmother in 978. When hunting in this area, Edward called at the castle. His stepmother brought him a cup of wine and, as he drank, one of her servants stabbed the king in the back. The slain monarch was canonised as Edward the Martyr, and Corfe Church was dedicated to his memory.

◆

CORFE CASTLE
The Cross 1899

When this photograph was taken at the very end of the 19th century, the cross celebrating Queen Victoria's' Diamond Jubilee had only been in place for two years, and Corfe was already busy with tourists. The establishment behind the cross provided tea, coffee, lemonade and ginger beer; a full tea, with food as well as drink, cost 6d.

CORFE CASTLE, THE CROSS 1890 43786

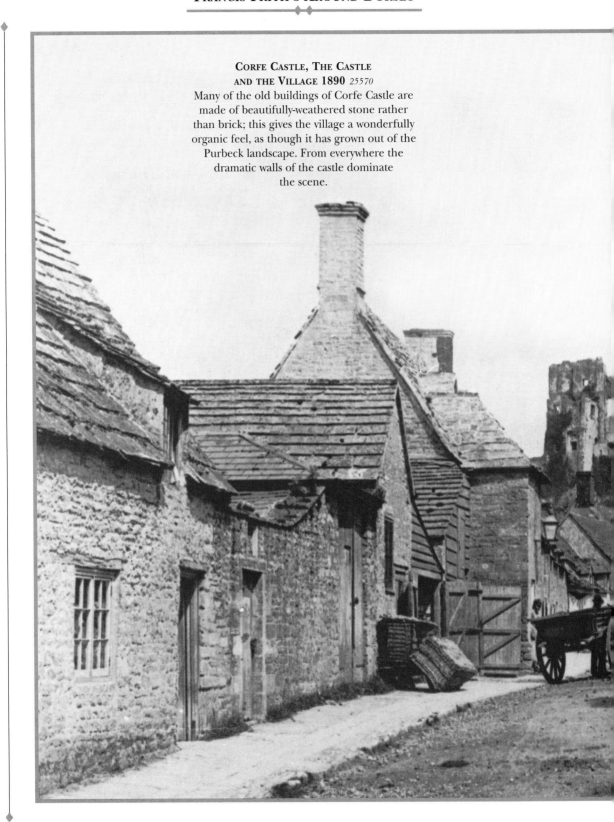

CORFE CASTLE, THE CASTLE
AND THE VILLAGE 1890 *25570*
Many of the old buildings of Corfe Castle are
made of beautifully-weathered stone rather
than brick; this gives the village a wonderfully
organic feel, as though it has grown out of the
Purbeck landscape. From everywhere the
dramatic walls of the castle dominate
the scene.

CORFE MULLEN, OLD MILL TEA ROOMS c1955 C596005
Corfe Mullen had a mill as long ago as the Domesday Book; it retained its independence until well into the 20th century, when its great neighbour Poole began to creep out towards it. Its greatest attraction, not shown here, is the delightful little 13th century church.

CRANBORNE, THE SQUARE c1955 C694010
Once at the heart of King John's hunting ground of Cranborne Chase, the village of Cranborne is rich in history. Its old manor house was a temporary refuge for Charles I at the height of the Civil War, and the parish church stands on the site of an important Saxon monastery.

CRANBORNE, WIMBORNE STREET c1955 C694013

CRANBORNE
Wimborne Street c1955

Thomas Hardy writes of a journey into Cranborne in 'Tess of the D'Urbervilles', where the present Fleur-de-Lys tavern is depicted as the much less salubrious 'Flower-de-Luce'. In the woodlands of the Chase, Tess is seduced by Alec D'Urberville, though Hardy's imagination makes the area much wilder than it would probably have been even in his day.

EVERSHOT
Fore Street c1965

Situated on the high downlands where the flowing waters of St John's Spring become the source of the River Frome, Evershot had as its vicar in the 18th century the poet George Crabbe. The award of the living allowed Crabbe to marry, though he seldom visited the parish, sending a curate in his stead.

EVERSHOT, FORE STREET c1965 E128015

FRAMPTON, THE VILLAGE 1906 54584
The rural poet William Barnes achieved
national fame through the endeavours of Mrs
Caroline Norton, who stayed here while the
Dorset bard was living nearby at
Winterbourne Came. Without her efforts,
Barnes might never have been known beyond
the bounds of his county.

FRAMPTON. THE CHURCH 1906 54585
Frampton, 'the settlement on the Frome', is an attractive downland village north-west of Dorchester. The old manor house of Frampton Court was demolished in 1939. In 1840 its then owner dismantled a large portion of the village to improve his view. There is a delicious irony in the fact that the village has now survived his house.

FROME VAUCHURCH, THE VILLAGE 1906 54575
This attractive waterside village was the home of the novelist and poet Sylvia Townsend Warner for over forty years. Its tiny towerless church stands sentinel over the cottages, gardens and meadows as it has done for some eight hundred years.

GODMANSTONE, THE SMITHS ARMS C1955 G179003
Once the village smithy, the inn at Godmanstone is said to be the smallest public house in England. The beautifully-thatched building measures only 20 ft by 10 ft; it is about 500 years old.

HAZELBURY BRYAN, THE POST OFFICE C1955 H294007
This village sprawls around the lanes of the surrounding countryside of the Blackmoor Vale as though not quite sure where it wants to be. The hilltop church dates back to at least the 14th century, and some of the cottages are of similar antiquity.

HILTON, THE VILLAGE c1955 H158004
Two miles south of Bulbarrow, one of Dorset's highest summits, Hilton and neighbouring Milton Abbas share some of the most beautiful countryside in the county. The thatched cottages, fascinating church and wonderful landscapes make Hilton a delightful place to linger.

HOLDENHURST, THE VILLAGE GREEN c1955 H296007
Now more or less a suburb of Bournemouth, and with some ugly new development, Holdenhurst's best attraction is its green, which has somehow managed to survive the urban sprawl threatening to engulf the rest of the surrounding countryside.

LANGTON MATRAVERS
The Kings Arms and High Street c1965

Once largely occupied by stoneworkers from the nearby stone quarries, this village stretches along the highway for a considerable distance, hence its name, a corruption of 'Longtown'. The Matravers family were considerable landowners on the Isle of Purbeck, and one Matravers was bloodily involved in the murder of Edward II.

◆

LITTON CHENEY
The Village 1906

Litton Cheney has a charming collection of Stuart and Georgian cottages strung out along its winding streets. Tiny brooks fill the air with the sound of running water. Its church is a fascinating medieval survival, which somehow escaped the worst excesses of Victorian restorers.

LANGTON MATRAVERS, THE KINGS ARMS AND HIGH STREET c1965
L469032

LITTON CHENEY, THE VILLAGE 1906 54543

LODERS, THE VILLAGE 1903 50496
Loders was built in the domain of a Benedictine Priory founded by the Norman grandee Baldwin de Redvers during the reign of Henry I. The present parish church formerly served the priory; the beautiful gardens of Loders Court surround the church.

MAIDEN NEWTON, HIGH WEST STREET 1906 54562
Maiden Newton stands on the high road between Dorchester and Crewkerne, probably on a very old route between Dorset and Somerset. Too many motorists speed by, missing the best parts of this large village on the confluence of the rivers Frome and Hooke.

MAIDEN NEWTON, THE VILLAGE 1906 54567
The working lives of the Dorset labourers who lived in cottages like these was hard, with poor wages and long hours. One of Thomas Hardy's few forays into politics was to champion the cause of better treatment for rural workers.

MAIDEN NEWTON, THE MILL 1906 54570
Maiden Newton's mill is probably situated on the site of many earlier mill buildings. There are records of settlements here dating back to the Roman occupation. This mill became a carpet factory in the 20th century.

MAIDEN NEWTON, DORCHESTER ROAD 1906 54563

MAIDEN NEWTON
Dorchester Road 1906
Maiden Newton makes a good centre for exploring the Dorset downs. Many visitors walk up to the Iron Age hillfort of Eggardon. One such rambler was Thomas Hardy, who famously used the ramparts as a setting in his novel 'The Trumpet Major'.

◆

MELBURY OSMOND
The Post Office c1955
Melbury Osmond is mentioned in the Domesday Book as belonging to the Arundell family. It stayed in their possession until about a century ago. Thomas Hardy's parents were married in the village church in 1839.

MELBURY OSMOND, THE POST OFFICE c1955 M216004

MELPLASH, THE CHURCH AND THE SCHOOL 1907 58148
Melplash church may look vaguely Norman in design, but in fact it is less than two hundred years old. Unkind visitors have commented that the stout building resembles a water tower!

MELPLASH, THE VILLAGE 1912 65063
Melplash's only real claim on history is the story of Sir Thomas More (a distant relative of the saint): when he was Sheriff of Dorset, he freed all the prisoners from Dorchester gaol. More had to give both Melplash and his favourite daughter to Lord Paulet, who interceded with the king on his behalf in search of a pardon.

MILTON ABBAS, THE VILLAGE C1955 M80049

When the first Earl of Dorchester purchased Milton Abbey in 1752, he had the entire village dismantled, moving it further away from his new home. The picturesque village we see today with its carefully-tended gardens is the result of his quest for privacy.

MORCOMBELAKE, THE VILLAGE 1904 52774

Morcombelake, situated on the high road between Lyme Regis and Bridport, is now famous as the home of the Moore's biscuit factory. The village itself is unjustly ignored by most travellers, who would do well to halt awhile to explore its buildings and the delightful countryside nearby.

MORE CRICHEL
Crichel House 1904

Princess Charlotte, the only child of the loveless marriage between George IV and Caroline of Brunswick, made Crichel House her home for a time. This popular princess died at the age of 21. Had she lived, she would have been Queen of England instead of Victoria, and the whole course of world history would have been different.

◆

MORETON
The Post Office c1955

Moreton is the last resting place of Lawrence of Arabia, who lived nearby at Cloud's Hill. He died on the Bovington road in May 1935 riding his beloved motorcycle. Seventy years later, pilgrims still make the journey to pay homage at his grave.

MORE CRICHEL, CRICHEL HOUSE 1904 52745

MORETON, THE POST OFFICE c1955 M308008

PUDDLETOWN, ATHELHAMPTON HALL c1955 P163046
Athelhampton Hall is one of two grand houses near to the village of Puddletown, both lived in at various times by members of the Martyn family. The village church has many memorials to this longstanding local family.

PUDDLETOWN, HIGH STREET c1955 P163043
Puddletown is the 'Weatherbury' of Thomas Hardy's 'Far From the Madding Crowd'. This area is rich in Hardy associations. Much of Puddletown was rebuilt in 1864, but the area around the church suggests the village that the young Hardy would have known.

SIXPENNY HANDLEY
Main Street c1955

Sixpenny Handley, at the heart of Cranborne Chase, has always had an air of outlawry. This was the home of the notorious smuggler Isaac Gulliver, who made the inn the focus of his trading activities during the 18th century. In the next century, it achieved further notoriety as the home of numerous poaching gangs.

◆

SIXPENNY HANDLEY
The Pond and the Vicarage c1955

This is a timeless photograph. This fine study of a horse and cart at Handley Pond portrays a rural scene that could have been observed at any period during the last several centuries.

SIXPENNY HANDLEY, MAIN STREET c1955   H460002

SIXPENNY HANDLEY, THE POND AND THE VICARAGE c1955   H460006

TOLPUDDLE, MAIN STREET c1955 T154026

Tolpuddle will always be an important place in English history. From here six farm labourers were transported to Australia in 1834 for taking an illegal oath in their quest for union recognition and better wages and conditions. This harsh treatment shocked the world, eventually winning the Martyrs a pardon which allowed them to come home.

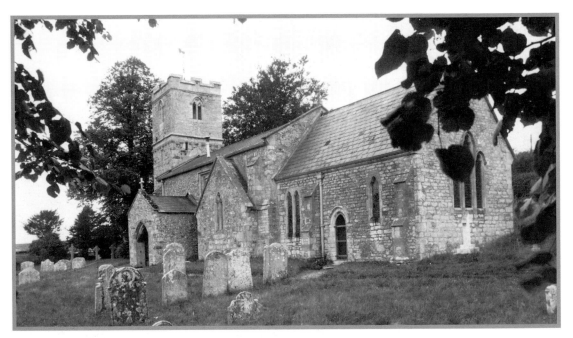

TOLPUDDLE, THE CHURCH c1955 T154010

Though restored in 1855, the church at Tolpuddle is nine centuries old. In the north transept is a memorial carved in Purbeck stone to a 12th century priest called Phillip. In the churchyard is the last resting place of James Hammett, the only Tolpuddle Martyr to return to live in his home village.

WITCHAMPTON, THE VILLAGE 1904 52739

This fine brick-built village is one of north Dorset's loveliest, its cottage gardens a delight all year round. Even with modern day traffic it seems a place lost in time. Its devotees return again and again.

WITCHAMPTON, THE MILL 1904 52742

The mill at Witchampton stands on the site of a much older mill building. This would have been a familiar view for Carr John Glyn, rector of the village from 1829 to 1896, one of the longest serving parish priests on record.

As you journey eastwards from the sedate and literary little town of Lyme Regis towards the sandy beaches and urban sprawl of Bournemouth, you become aware that this beautiful Dorset coast has been created by the happy amalgamation of the best of nature and the sympathetic handling of the original creation by humankind, for this is very much a worked landscape. Generations of farmers have grazed and tilled the ground, but much more gently than in many parts of England, using methods not so different from those used by their distant ancestors. The coastline, though, is largely still in the hands of nature, and is still being shaped by erosion and the power of the sea.

Towns such as Weymouth and Poole have grown up around shipping and fishing, their seamen going out to brave the rough tides and wild seas of the English Channel. Portland and Purbeck, both really peninsulas, not islands, bear the marks of the quarrymen who have wrought out tons of stone, not only for local buildings but for distant landmarks such as St Paul's Cathedral. Yet these parts of Dorset bear their scars proudly, like battle honours rather than as a despoliation.

Despite the occasional intrusion of a holiday camp or caravan park, the coast remains unspoiled between the major towns. Waves still crash on the long and lonely shingle of Chesil Beach, just as J Meade Faulkner described it in his Victorian smuggling romance 'Moonfleet'. Beyond this huge ridge of stones is the Fleet itself, that strange lake of brackish water that begins at Abbotsbury, where it is white with swans, to its end against the narrow isthmus where the Isle of Portland meets the mainland.

Unlike neighbouring Devon, there are no great estuaries on this coastline, though the wide expanse of Poole Harbour gives welcome shelter to yachts. The harbours at Lyme

Regis and West Bay are artificial constructions, won back from the sea to facilitate trade and the safety of shipping. Fishing villages such as Studland cling to the coast; below them are the beaches of sand and shingle where fishing families have launched their boats from generation to generation.

Weymouth and Poole are still important ports, and have become resorts by mere fluke. Bournemouth, on the other hand, was almost purposely built to cater for tourists, from Lewis Tregonwell, who built the first holiday home there in 1810, to the tourist flats and hotels of today. This huge town has now dwarfed its ancient neighbour Christchurch. But both Bournemouth and Christchurch are really cuckoos in the nest, belonging still in spirit, as they once did in actuality, to neighbouring Hampshire.

Each coastal town has charm and individuality; it would be difficult to confuse one with any other, so much are they distinct in character and style. They are a taste of Dorset at its best, and the discerning visitor will savour the chance to linger and explore.

LYME REGIS, THE HARBOUR 1892 31308
When the nearby harbour of Axmouth fell into disuse after a cliff-fall in the 12th century, the nearest alternative was to extend the harbour at Lyme. In 1582 the topographer Roger North exclaimed 'There is not any harbour like it in the world'. At the time this picture was taken, hundreds of ships were using Lyme's harbour each year.

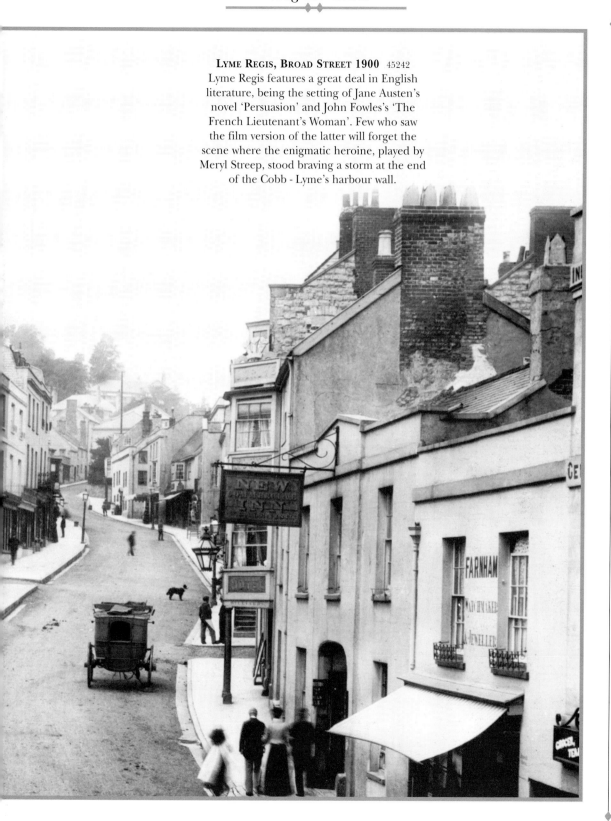

LYME REGIS, BROAD STREET 1900 45242
Lyme Regis features a great deal in English literature, being the setting of Jane Austen's novel 'Persuasion' and John Fowles's 'The French Lieutenant's Woman'. Few who saw the film version of the latter will forget the scene where the enigmatic heroine, played by Meryl Streep, stood braving a storm at the end of the Cobb - Lyme's harbour wall.

LYME REGIS, SHERBORNE LANE 1907 58099
Sherborne Lane is shown here when the
Crown and Anchor, the large building at the
foot of the hill, was still open. This is
probably the oldest part of Lyme, being built
on land given to Sherborne Abbey in 744 by
King Cynewulf, king of Wessex.

LYME REGIS, IN THE LANES 1892 31311
These old tracks from the neighbouring village of Uplyme were the original routes into the town before the present coast road was constructed. Along these, packhorses would bring wool for export, the Duke of Monmouth's rebels marched and Jane Austen perhaps gained her first glimpse of Lyme.

LYME REGIS
Buddle Bridge 1922

Buddle Bridge straddles the River Lim just as its running waters meet the sea. This river travels only a short journey from above Uplyme, and runs under many bridges as it threads its way through the town. The bridge itself is one of Lyme's oldest, being mostly medieval beneath its modern strengthening.

◆

LYME REGIS
Cannington Viaduct 1903

Lyme Regis was relatively late in having the advantage of its own railway line, for its station opened only in 1903. Cannington Viaduct, near Uplyme, was one of the first railway bridges to be made out of concrete. The railway link to the town was severed in the 1960s.

LYME REGIS, BUDDLE BRIDGE 1922 72770

LYME REGIS, CANNINGTON VIADUCT 1903 50253

CHIDEOCK, THE VILLAGE 1912 65080
Chideock, always pronounced without the 'e', is set in a landscape of ancient ridgeways and rolling hills. Its charming cottages witnessed some of the fiercest fighting of the English Civil War, and its narrow streets some of the most daring smuggling escapades of recent centuries.

CHIDEOCK, THE VILLAGE 1922 72804
Many of the buildings in Chideock are thatched and built of the warm local yellow sandstone which, despite modern traffic, makes this pretty village well worth a visit. In the aftermath of the Great War, the post office still bears a recruiting poster. It is interesting to speculate whether the 'Local Views' in the postcard rack are by the Frith company.

BURTON BRADSTOCK, THE VILLAGE 1902 48412

BURTON BRADSTOCK
The Village 1902

Henry I gave the village and living of Burton Bradstock to the great Normandy abbey at Caen in exchange for the royal regalia of William the Conqueror, which the monks claimed had been gifted to them by the dying king. This lovely village was considered a reasonable exchange for England's crown jewels.

◆

BURTON BRADSTOCK
The Beach 1930

Such is the unbroken nature of the West Dorset coastline that artificial harbours had to be constructed at Lyme Regis and West Bay. The small coves between, such as the beach below Burton Bradstock, would be used mostly by local fishermen and smugglers.

BURTON BRADSTOCK, THE BEACH 1930 83366

ABBOTSBURY
The Tithe Barn 1890
Abbotsbury, situated at the western end of Chesil Beach, is most famous for its swannery, the waters of the Fleet often being turned white with hundreds of birds. But for centuries the village was the location of a substantial monastery. Only a few ruins and the tithe barn remain.

◆

PORTLAND
Chesil Beach 1890
Chesil Beach, seen here from the Isle of Portland, is a great ridge of shingle eight miles long, with a lagoon of brackish water between it and the mainland. Its stones tend to be much larger at one end than the other. John Meade Faulkner immortalised the area in his famous smuggling novel 'Moonfleet'.

ABBOTSBURY, THE TITHE BARN 1890 27322

PORTLAND, CHESIL BEACH 1890 27328

PORTLAND
Rufus Castle 1890

The ruins of the Norman castle, probably named Rufus after the second Norman king, is situated high above Church Ope Cove. The building is known to locals as Bow and Arrow Castle; Portland's old parish church, ruined by landslides, is within its grounds.

◆

PORTLAND
Fortuneswell 1894

The Isle's main town of Fortuneswell grew up, as the name implies, around a supply of fresh water, as did many of the Portland settlements. On this barren rock, surrounded by salt water, such wells were hard to come by and exploited to the full when they were.

PORTLAND, RUFUS CASTLE 1890 27335

PORTLAND, FORTUNESWELL 1894 34550

PORTLAND, STREET SCENE 1894 34551

Castleton, Fortuneswell and Chesil now form the largest urban settlement where the Isle meets the causeway from the mainland. When this photograph was taken, they were three discreet villages, overlooking the great naval base in one direction and being overlooked by the convict prison from the other.

PORTLAND, THE PRISON ENTRANCE 1898 41146

Portland prison was a grim institution during Victoria's reign, with convicts spending long days breaking stone in the nearby quarries with pickaxe and crowbar. Well-behaved prisoners were allowed the privilege of maintaining the prison gardens.

PORTLAND, GENERAL VIEW 1898 41142

PORTLAND
General View 1898
The Isle of Portland is more properly a peninsula, which Thomas Hardy described as 'The Gibraltar of Wessex'. It is a harsh and unforgiving landscape, but a place of considerable charm to those who seek out its quiet corners and hidden delights.

◆

WEYMOUTH
Sandsfoot Castle 1898
Sandsfoot Castle, now tumbling into the sea, was built by Henry VIII to guard the sea-lanes between Weymouth and Portland. The Tudor topographer Leland described it as being 'a right goodlie and warlyke castle'. It changed hands several times during the Civil War, before finally falling into ruin in the 1700s.

WEYMOUTH, SANDSFOOT CASTLE 1898 41138

WEYMOUTH, THE ESPLANADE 1899 43852
Weymouth became popular as a seaside resort thanks to the patronage of George III, who came to bathe here for the good of his health. As the king plunged into the waves a brass band, discreetly hidden in a bathing machine, played God Save the King!

WEYMOUTH, THE PARADE 1904 52858
An old guidebook stressed the benefits to health of a holiday in Weymouth: 'Weymouth is much more open than the majority of seaside resorts, and is almost surrounded by salt water. This results in an air largely impregnated with ozone and, with the ever-changing tide, ensures a constantly renewed atmosphere'.

WEYMOUTH
The Pier and the Pavilion 1909
Weymouth esplanade winds round to the pier and pavilion theatre, a favourite stroll for the Edwardian visitors seen here. The pier at this time was 1050 feet long, and was a favoured location for watching the steamers come in and out. In 1909 the admission fee for the pier was 2d.

WEYMOUTH
The Pavilion 1909
The Pavilion Theatre was a year old when this photograph was taken. The new entertainment venue quickly eclipsed the other small halls around the town, offering a variety of plays all the year round to an audience of up to 1100 people.

WEYMOUTH, THE PIER AND THE PAVILION 1909 61589

WEYMOUTH, THE PAVILION 1909 61594

WEYMOUTH, THE SANDS 1918 68116
It was the early use of bathing machines that made Weymouth such a popular resort for sea bathing. The larger machines shown here ran down to the water on rails, and had a number of cubicles. Affluent visitors would hire single-cubicle machines for themselves.

LULWORTH, DURDLE DOOR 1894 34583

The great natural arch of Durdle Door braves the sea just a little way from the more famous Lulworth Cove. The beautiful surrounding coastline is lonely and unspoiled once the roads and traffic are left behind.

LULWORTH, THE COVE 1894 34569

To the left, an artist sits at an easel and paints Lulworth Cove, while his wife shades herself with a parasol. By the end of the 19th century, the cove was already attracting a great many visitors. Its perfect natural harbour, hollowed out by the Channel into its present near-circular form, is one of the most distinctive bays on the English coastline.

LULWORTH, THE BEACH AND A STEAMER C1955 L112021
The beauty of Lulworth Cove has always attracted writers and artists. John Keats spent some of his last days in England here, as did Rupert Brooke. Thomas Hardy immortalised the cove in novels and poems, while artistic views are on sale in every Dorset gallery and gift shop.

LULWORTH, THE COVE RESTAURANT C1955 L112016
By the 1950s Lulworth had become one of the most popular day excursions on the south coast, with cars and coaches jamming its narrow lanes. But for the walker and out-of-season visitor, the area retains the magic and beauty that earlier visitors would have enjoyed.

SWANAGE
Tilly Whim Caves 1894
Tilly Whim Caves, on the coast west of Swanage, are a strange mixture of quarrying and erosion. They were an attraction noted by early guidebook writers, who nevertheless deplored the graffiti carved into the rock by Victorian trippers.

◆

SWANAGE
The Beach 1899
Thomas Hardy described Swanage as '...a seaside village, lying snugly within two headlands as between a finger and thumb'. The town may get its name from Swene's Wic, the Bay of Swene, perhaps commemorating the great naval battle fought nearby between the Saxons and Danes in 877.

SWANAGE, TILLY WHIM CAVES 1894 34608

SWANAGE, THE BEACH 1899 43762

SWANAGE, THE COASTGUARD STATION 1897 40310
For hundreds of years smuggling was a major industry in Swanage: the smuggled goods were hidden in the local caves and quarries. Prominent coastguard stations were built along the coast to act as a deterrent.

SWANAGE, FROM THE COASTGUARD STATION 1897 40308
Swanage pier is really a jetty, 28 feet wide and 1,400 feet long. In 1897 the pier would have been used either to give access to the many passenger steamers that plied their trade along the coast or to transport the famous Purbeck stone on merchant ships.

SWANAGE
The Pier 1897
Bathing was permitted from Swanage
pier on weekdays from 6-8am and on
Sundays from 7-9am. A modest charge
was made to anyone who wished
to indulge.

◆

SWANAGE
From the Pier 1897
Carriages are drawn up on the approach
to the pier to collect passengers from
the arriving steamers. Elsewhere,
strollers pay their pennies to come
through the turnstile to walk the pier
and sample the balmy sea air.

SWANAGE, THE PIER 1897 40306

SWANAGE, FROM THE PIER 1897 40305

STUDLAND, THE NEW INN 1890 25557

Studland's most famous resident was Sergeant William Lawrence, who fought with Wellington in Spain and at Waterloo. He spent his retirement running the village inn with his French wife Clothilde. Both now rest in the churchyard.

STUDLAND, THE BEACH 1925 78796

The attraction of Studland is not only the attractive beach and picturesque coastal scenery, but also the wild heathland around the village. Studland Heath is now a national nature reserve, famous for the variety of its birdlife.

BROWNSEA ISLAND, THE CASTLE 1891 29621

Brownsea is the largest island in Poole Harbour, and now belongs to the National Trust. In 1907, Robert Baden Powell held a camp for boys on the island, which laid the foundations for the Boy Scout movement.

BROWNSEA ISLAND, THE CASTLE 1891 29623

A castle was first erected on Brownsea Island by Henry VIII, and was strengthened at the time of the Armada. The present building was largely the work of the Victorian Colonel Waugh, who developed the island by opening clay pits and potteries in its wildest corners.

POOLE, THE TOWN CELLARS 1887 19511

Poole's Town Cellars, in the heart of Poole's mercantile district, are seen here on a busy day . The town had many independent breweries at this time; here we see one of their horse-drawn drays preparing for a delivery round.

POOLE, THE HARBOUR OFFICES 1904 52815

Close to the quays at Poole is the 18th-century harbour office, once the Old Town House, a club for ships' captains. On the front of the building is an old sundial, and on the side a carving of Benjamin Skutt, Mayor of Poole in 1727.

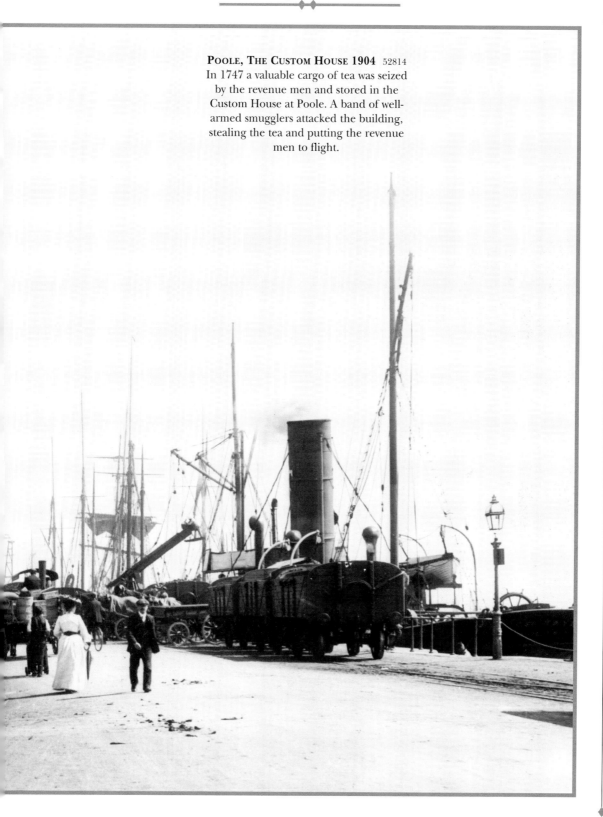

POOLE, THE CUSTOM HOUSE 1904 52814
In 1747 a valuable cargo of tea was seized by the revenue men and stored in the Custom House at Poole. A band of well-armed smugglers attacked the building, stealing the tea and putting the revenue men to flight.

POOLE, HIGH STREET 1900 46088
Poole developed alongside the finest natural harbour in England; it still maintains strong links with the sea, having become a mecca for yachtsmen. The prosperous town, built where the sea meets the wild heathlands of Dorset, is one of the largest on England's south coast.

POOLE, HIGH STREET 1904 52807
Poole did not become a holiday resort for many years, but retained its importance as a port and merchant centre. By 1904 holidaymakers were discovering the delights of the locality, and some of the sandier areas of Poole Harbour were attracting bathers.

BOURNEMOUTH, FROM SOUTHBOURNE TERRACE c1870 5500

Bournemouth, once in Hampshire but now in Dorset, did not exist two hundred years ago. In 1810, Lewis Tregonwell built a holiday home on lonely heathland, close to the mouth of the River Bourne. Other wealthy gentlemen followed his example, but it was to be towards the middle of that century before the town achieved popularity as a holiday resort.

BOURNEMOUTH, THE ARCADE c1871 5511

As with so many seaside resorts of the 19th century, Bournemouth attracted a wealthy and fashionable clientele. Shopkeepers were not long in seeing the business potential of catering for both residents and tourists. Shops and arcades were opened in the centre of town, such as the splendid example of Victorian architecture shown here.

BOURNEMOUTH, FROM THE PIER 1897 40559
Less than a century after its foundation, the town was already dominating the skyline and its beaches were among the most crowded on the south coast. Thomas Hardy immortalised the town as 'the city of detached mansions' in 'Tess of the D'Urbervilles'.

BOURNEMOUTH, FROM WEST CLIFF 1897 40553
Bournemouth pier stands above the original mouth of the River Bourne. Its construction marked the town's commitment to its role as a resort. The mildness of the climate first attracted tourists to the town, and it rapidly acquired a reputation as a health resort beneficial to consumptives.

BOURNEMOUTH, THE METROPOLE HOTEL 1900 45227
Luxury hotels were built to cater for the better-heeled visitor to Bournemouth, prospering until well into the 20th century. Some early tourists would hire villas and bring their entire family and retinue of servants with them.

BOURNEMOUTH, THE SQUARE 1900 45218

Bournemouth's Square stands at the very heart of the town astride the River Bourne. Here we see the carriages of the wealthy assembled and waiting to take their clients back to their hotels and villas.

BOURNEMOUTH, THE PIER ENTRANCE 1925 78768

A view of busy Bournemouth pier, attracting strollers and sightseers. The pier has undergone several transformations since it was first built, but retains its popularity. By the 1920s cars had almost completely replaced horse-drawn carriages, and charabanc tours had become a popular feature of a seaside holiday.

BOSCOMBE, THE ARCADE 1892 31380

BOSCOMBE
The Arcade 1892
Bournemouth rapidly absorbed the older settlement of Boscombe. Its shops and arcades attracted visitors from its larger neighbour. The gothic architecture seen here remained an enthusiasm for builders and architects throughout the Victorian period.

◆

BOSCOMBE
From the Pier 1900
Boscombe developed to the east of Bournemouth in mid-Victorian times, attracting the wealthy and fashionable. Mineral springs added to Boscombe's attraction for those seeking an improvement to health, though it never became the spa it aspired to be.

BOSCOMBE, FROM THE PIER 1900 45232

BOSCOMBE
In the Chine 1903

Boscombe was built across a wooded chine, a wide ravine, that leads down to the sea; chines are common on this coast. Many of the quieter strolls have by now been turned into formal gardens, where tourists and locals alike can sit and contemplate the scenery on pleasant days.

BOSCOMBE
The Pier 1903

Like Bournemouth's pier, the structure at Boscombe was severely damaged in the Second World War, but both have been sympathetically restored. A third pier at Southbourne did not survive.

BOSCOMBE, IN THE CHINE 1903 49160

BOSCOMBE, THE PIER 1903 49156

BOSCOMBE, FROM THE PIER 1903 49158
In this view we see a busy scene of an
Edwardian seaside beach with paddlers,
bathing machines and towels for hire. As at
Bournemouth, the houses stand back from
unstable cliffs with steep paths zigzagging
down to provide access to the sands.

SOUTHBOURNE, THE PROMENADE c1955 S153123
Southbourne stands above the seven miles of golden beaches that attract the tourist again and again to this part of the coast; a cliff railway facilitates access to the sands. By the 1950s, Southbourne had been almost completely swallowed up by the expanding Bournemouth district.

SOUTHBOURNE, STREET SCENE C1955 S153101

Southbourne has an unfortunate place in aviation history as the scene of the air crash that killed the pioneer pilot Mr Rolls, of Rolls Royce fame, in 1910. Rolls was the first person to die in a British air accident.

HIGHCLIFFE CASTLE, NEAR CHRISTCHURCH 1900 45059

Highcliffe Castle was once one of the grandest stately homes in southern England. Restoration is bringing it back to its former glory. The Grade I listed building was built by Lord Stuart de Rothesay in the Romantic style between 1830 and 1835; he employed the fashionable London architect William Donthorpe.

HIGHCLIFFE, LYMINGTON ROAD c1955 H295017

Highcliffe is the most easterly parish in Dorset, famous for eroding cliffs and splendid views across to the Isle of Wight. The 1950s were the last profitable heyday of the small and diverse local shop, before the supermarkets changed British shopping habits for ever. Lymington Road at this period had a wide selection of different traders to satisfy local demand.

CHRISTCHURCH, WICK FERRY 1900 45045

A peaceful scene at Wick Ferry, close to Christchurch. Even then, tourists were flocking to such picturesque places by foot, cycle, carriage and boat. This has developed into the massive crowds that flock nowadays into this area on hot summer days.

CHRISTCHURCH, THE RIVER STOUR 1918 68054

The ancient town of Christchurch stands on the two rivers Stour and Avon, getting its old name Twyneham from the Anglo-Saxon, meaning 'the town between two rivers'. Not far beyond the town the journey through Dorset ends as the boundary of Hampshire is reached.

THOMAS HARDY'S DORSET VIEWS

Many of the places illustrated by the Frith family of photographers in Dorset would have been familiar to the poet and novelist Thomas Hardy. Hardy was born at Higher Bockhampton, near Stinsford, in 1840, working as an architect before achieving fame as a writer. In his famous Wessex series of novels, and in his poetry, he portrayed Dorset's countryside, towns and villages in detail, peopling them with the kind of country people he would have grown up with. Hardy left a fine legacy of novels, such as 'Far From the Madding Crowd', 'The Mayor of Casterbridge', 'The Trumpet-Major', 'Under the Greenwood Tree' and 'Tess of the D'Urbervilles', which are set firmly in a slightly-fictionalised Dorset landscape. As the 20th century dawned, Hardy abandoned novel writing in favour of poetry. He died at Max Gate, his home near Dorchester, in 1928.

It is possible to compare the Dorset portrayed by both Hardy and Frith by using the key below. On the left are Hardy's fictional Wessex place-names, on the right the geographical names as mentioned in this book.

Anglebury **Wareham**

Budmouth **Weymouth**

Casterbridge **Dorchester**

Chalk Newton **Maiden Newton**

The Chase **Cranborne Chase**

Chaseborough **Cranborne**

Chene Manor **Canford Manor**

Corvesgate Castle **Corfe Castle**

Emminster **Beaminster**

Evershead **Evershot**

Havenpool **Poole**

Isle of Slingers **Portland**

King Henry VIII's Castle **Sandsfoot Castle**

Knollsea **Swanage**

Leddenton **Gillingham**

Little Hintock **Melbury Osmond**

Lulstead **Lulworth**

Mellstock **Stinsford**

Norcombe **Eggardon Hill**

Nuzzleberry **Hazelbury Bryan**

Port Bredy **Bridport**

Sandbourne **Bournemouth**

Shaston **Shaftesbury**

Sherton Abbas **Sherborne**

Shottsford Forum **Blandford Forum**

Southerton **Wareham**

The Street of Wells **Fortuneswell**

Tolchurch **Tolpuddle**

Warborne **Wimborne Minster**

Weatherbury **Puddletown**

Well-Bridge **Wool**

Index

Abbotsbury 82

Allington 43

Badbury Rings 38

Beaminster 44, 45, 46

Bindon Abbey 46

Blandford Forum, 39, 40-41

Boscombe 108, 109, 110-111

Bournemouth 103, 104-105, 106, 107

Bovington 47

Bradpole 48

Bridport 21, 22-23, 24, 25

Brownsea Island 98

Burton Bradstock 81

Canford Manor 48

Castle Corfe Castle 50, 51, 52-53

Charminster 49, 50

Chideock 80

Christchurch 114, 115

Corfe 50, 51, 52-53

Corfe Mullen 54

Cranborne 54, 55

Dorchester 14, 15, 16-17, 18, 19, 20

Evershot 55

Frampton 56-57, 58

Frome Vauchurch 58

Godmanstone 59

Hazelbury Bryan 59

Highcliffe 113, 114

Higher Bockhampton 20

Hilton 60

Holdenhurst 60

Langton Matravers 61

Litton Cheney 61

Loders 62

Lulworth 92, 93

Lyme Regis 73, 74-75, 76-77, 78, 79

Maiden Newton 62, 63, 64

Melbury Osmond 64

Melplash 65

Milton Abbas 66

Morcombelake 66

More Crichel 67

Moreton 67

Poole 99, 100-101, 102,

Portland 82, 83, 84, 85

Puddletown 68

Shaftesbury 25, 26

Sherborne 27, 28, 29

Sixpenny Handley 69

Southbourne 112, 113

Studland 97

Swanage 94, 95, 96

Tolpuddle 70

Wareham 30-31, 32

Weymouth 85, 86-87, 88, 89, 90-91

Wimborne 32, 33, 34, 35, 36-37

Wimborne Minster 32, 33, 34

Witchampton 71

Frith Book Co Titles

www.francisfrith.co.uk

The Frith Book Company publishes over 100 new titles each year. A selection of those currently available are listed below. For latest catalogue please contact Frith Book Co.

Town Books 96 pages, approx 100 photos. County and Themed Books 128 pages, approx 150 photos (unless specified). All titles hardback laminated case and jacket except those indicated pb (paperback)

Amersham, Chesham & Rickmansworth (pb)			Derby (pb)	1-85937-367-4	£9.99
	1-85937-340-2	£9.99	Derbyshire (pb)	1-85937-196-5	£9.99
Ancient Monuments & Stone Circles	1-85937-143-4	£17.99	Devon (pb)	1-85937-297-x	£9.99
Aylesbury (pb)	1-85937-227-9	£9.99	Dorset (pb)	1-85937-269-4	£9.99
Bakewell	1-85937-113-2	£12.99	Dorset Churches	1-85937-172-8	£17.99
Barnstaple (pb)	1-85937-300-3	£9.99	Dorset Coast (pb)	1-85937-299-6	£9.99
Bath (pb)	1-85937419-0	£9.99	Dorset Living Memories	1-85937-210-4	£14.99
Bedford (pb)	1-85937-205-8	£9.99	Down the Severn	1-85937-118-3	£14.99
Berkshire (pb)	1-85937-191-4	£9.99	Down the Thames (pb)	1-85937-278-3	£9.99
Berkshire Churches	1-85937-170-1	£17.99	Down the Trent	1-85937-311-9	£14.99
Blackpool (pb)	1-85937-382-8	£9.99	Dublin (pb)	1-85937-231-7	£9.99
Bognor Regis (pb)	1-85937-431-x	£9.99	East Anglia (pb)	1-85937-265-1	£9.99
Bournemouth	1-85937-067-5	£12.99	East London	1-85937-080-2	£14.99
Bradford (pb)	1-85937-204-x	£9.99	East Sussex	1-85937-130-2	£14.99
Brighton & Hove(pb)	1-85937-192-2	£8.99	Eastbourne	1-85937-061-6	£12.99
Bristol (pb)	1-85937-264-3	£9.99	Edinburgh (pb)	1-85937-193-0	£8.99
British Life A Century Ago (pb)	1-85937-213-9	£9.99	England in the 1880s	1-85937-331-3	£17.99
Buckinghamshire (pb)	1-85937-200-7	£9.99	English Castles (pb)	1-85937-434-4	£9.99
Camberley (pb)	1-85937-222-8	£9.99	English Country Houses	1-85937-161-2	£17.99
Cambridge (pb)	1-85937-422-0	£9.99	Essex (pb)	1-85937-270-8	£9.99
Cambridgeshire (pb)	1-85937-420-4	£9.99	Exeter	1-85937-126-4	£12.99
Canals & Waterways (pb)	1-85937-291-0	£9.99	Exmoor	1-85937-132-9	£14.99
Canterbury Cathedral (pb)	1-85937-179-5	£9.99	Falmouth	1-85937-066-7	£12.99
Cardiff (pb)	1-85937-093-4	£9.99	Folkestone (pb)	1-85937-124-8	£9.99
Carmarthenshire	1-85937-216-3	£14.99	Glasgow (pb)	1-85937-190-6	£9.99
Chelmsford (pb)	1-85937-310-0	£9.99	Gloucestershire	1-85937-102-7	£14.99
Cheltenham (pb)	1-85937-095-0	£9.99	Great Yarmouth (pb)	1-85937-426-3	£9.99
Cheshire (pb)	1-85937-271-6	£9.99	Greater Manchester (pb)	1-85937-266-x	£9.99
Chester	1-85937-090-x	£12.99	Guildford (pb)	1-85937-410-7	£9.99
Chesterfield	1-85937-378-x	£9.99	Hampshire (pb)	1-85937-279-1	£9.99
Chichester (pb)	1-85937-228-7	£9.99	Hampshire Churches (pb)	1-85937-207-4	£9.99
Colchester (pb)	1-85937-188-4	£8.99	Harrogate	1-85937-423-9	£9.99
Cornish Coast	1-85937-163-9	£14.99	Hastings & Bexhill (pb)	1-85937-131-0	£9.99
Cornwall (pb)	1-85937-229-5	£9.99	Heart of Lancashire (pb)	1-85937-197-3	£9.99
Cornwall Living Memories	1-85937-248-1	£14.99	Helston (pb)	1-85937-214-7	£9.99
Cotswolds (pb)	1-85937-230-9	£9.99	Hereford (pb)	1-85937-175-2	£9.99
Cotswolds Living Memories	1-85937-255-4	£14.99	Herefordshire	1-85937-174-4	£14.99
County Durham	1-85937-123-x	£14.99	Hertfordshire (pb)	1-85937-247-3	£9.99
Croydon Living Memories	1-85937-162-0	£9.99	Horsham (pb)	1-85937-432-8	£9.99
Cumbria	1-85937-101-9	£14.99	Humberside	1-85937-215-5	£14.99
Dartmoor	1-85937-145-0	£14.99	Hythe, Romney Marsh & Ashford	1-85937-256-2	£9.99

Available from your local bookshop or from the publisher

Frith Book Co Titles (continued)

Ipswich (pb)	1-85937-424-7	£9.99	St Ives (pb)	1-85937415-8	£9.99
Ireland (pb)	1-85937-181-7	£9.99	Scotland (pb)	1-85937-182-5	£9.99
Isle of Man (pb)	1-85937-268-6	£9.99	Scottish Castles (pb)	1-85937-323-2	£9.99
Isles of Scilly	1-85937-136-1	£14.99	Sevenoaks & Tunbridge	1-85937-057-8	£12.99
Isle of Wight (pb)	1-85937-429-8	£9.99	Sheffield, South Yorks (pb)	1-85937-267-8	£9.99
Isle of Wight Living Memories	1-85937-304-6	£14.99	Shrewsbury (pb)	1-85937-325-9	£9.99
Kent (pb)	1-85937-189-2	£9.99	Shropshire (pb)	1-85937-326-7	£9.99
Kent Living Memories	1-85937-125-6	£14.99	Somerset	1-85937-153-1	£14.99
Lake District (pb)	1-85937-275-9	£9.99	South Devon Coast	1-85937-107-8	£14.99
Lancaster, Morecambe & Heysham (pb)	1-85937-233-3	£9.99	South Devon Living Memories	1-85937-168-x	£14.99
Leeds (pb)	1-85937-202-3	£9.99	South Hams	1-85937-220-1	£14.99
Leicester	1-85937-073-x	£12.99	Southampton (pb)	1-85937-427-1	£9.99
Leicestershire (pb)	1-85937-185-x	£9.99	Southport (pb)	1-85937-425-5	£9.99
Lincolnshire (pb)	1-85937-433-6	£9.99	Staffordshire	1-85937-047-0	£12.99
Liverpool & Merseyside (pb)	1-85937-234-1	£9.99	Stratford upon Avon	1-85937-098-5	£12.99
London (pb)	1-85937-183-3	£9.99	Suffolk (pb)	1-85937-221-x	£9.99
Ludlow (pb)	1-85937-176-0	£9.99	Suffolk Coast	1-85937-259-7	£14.99
Luton (pb)	1-85937-235-x	£9.99	Surrey (pb)	1-85937-240-6	£9.99
Maidstone	1-85937-056-x	£14.99	Sussex (pb)	1-85937-184-1	£9.99
Manchester (pb)	1-85937-198-1	£9.99	Swansea (pb)	1-85937-167-1	£9.99
Middlesex	1-85937-158-2	£14.99	Tees Valley & Cleveland	1-85937-211-2	£14.99
New Forest	1-85937-128-0	£14.99	Thanet (pb)	1-85937-116-7	£9.99
Newark (pb)	1-85937-366-6	£9.99	Tiverton (pb)	1-85937-178-7	£9.99
Newport, Wales (pb)	1-85937-258-9	£9.99	Torbay	1-85937-063-2	£12.99
Newquay (pb)	1-85937-421-2	£9.99	Truro	1-85937-147-7	£12.99
Norfolk (pb)	1-85937-195-7	£9.99	Victorian and Edwardian Cornwall	1-85937-252-x	£14.99
Norfolk Living Memories	1-85937-217-1	£14.99	Victorian & Edwardian Devon	1-85937-253-8	£14.99
Northamptonshire	1-85937-150-7	£14.99	Victorian & Edwardian Kent	1-85937-149-3	£14.99
Northumberland Tyne & Wear (pb)	1-85937-281-3	£9.99	Vic & Ed Maritime Album	1-85937-144-2	£17.99
North Devon Coast	1-85937-146-9	£14.99	Victorian and Edwardian Sussex	1-85937-157-4	£14.99
North Devon Living Memories	1-85937-261-9	£14.99	Victorian & Edwardian Yorkshire	1-85937-154-x	£14.99
North London	1-85937-206-6	£14.99	Victorian Seaside	1-85937-159-0	£17.99
North Wales (pb)	1-85937-298-8	£9.99	Villages of Devon (pb)	1-85937-293-7	£9.99
North Yorkshire (pb)	1-85937-236-8	£9.99	Villages of Kent (pb)	1-85937-294-5	£9.99
Norwich (pb)	1-85937-194-9	£8.99	Villages of Sussex (pb)	1-85937-295-3	£9.99
Nottingham (pb)	1-85937-324-0	£9.99	Warwickshire (pb)	1-85937-203-1	£9.99
Nottinghamshire (pb)	1-85937-187-6	£9.99	Welsh Castles (pb)	1-85937-322-4	£9.99
Oxford (pb)	1-85937-411-5	£9.99	West Midlands (pb)	1-85937-289-9	£9.99
Oxfordshire (pb)	1-85937-430-1	£9.99	West Sussex	1-85937-148-5	£14.99
Peak District (pb)	1-85937-280-5	£9.99	West Yorkshire (pb)	1-85937-201-5	£9.99
Penzance	1-85937-069-1	£12.99	Weymouth (pb)	1-85937-209-0	£9.99
Peterborough (pb)	1-85937-219-8	£9.99	Wiltshire (pb)	1-85937-277-5	£9.99
Piers	1-85937-237-6	£17.99	Wiltshire Churches (pb)	1-85937-171-x	£9.99
Plymouth	1-85937-119-1	£12.99	Wiltshire Living Memories	1-85937-245-7	£14.99
Poole & Sandbanks (pb)	1-85937-251-1	£9.99	Winchester (pb)	1-85937-428-x	£9.99
Preston (pb)	1-85937-212-0	£9.99	Windmills & Watermills	1-85937-242-2	£17.99
Reading (pb)	1-85937-238-4	£9.99	Worcester (pb)	1-85937-165-5	£9.99
Romford (pb)	1-85937-319-4	£9.99	Worcestershire	1-85937-152-3	£14.99
Salisbury (pb)	1-85937-239-2	£9.99	York (pb)	1-85937-199-x	£9.99
Scarborough (pb)	1-85937-379-8	£9.99	Yorkshire (pb)	1-85937-186-8	£9.99
St Albans (pb)	1-85937-341-0	£9.99	Yorkshire Living Memories	1-85937-166-3	£14.99

See Frith books on the internet www.francisfrith.co.uk

FRITH PRODUCTS & SERVICES

Francis Frith would doubtless be pleased to know that the pioneering publishing venture he started in 1860 still continues today. A hundred and forty years later, The Francis Frith Collection continues in the same innovative tradition and is now one of the foremost publishers of vintage photographs in the world. Some of the current activities include:

Interior Decoration

Today Frith's photographs can be seen framed and as giant wall murals in thousands of pubs, restaurants, hotels, banks, retail stores and other public buildings throughout the country. In every case they enhance the unique local atmosphere of the places they depict and provide reminders of gentler days in an increasingly busy and frenetic world.

Product Promotions

Frith products are used by many major companies to promote the sales of their own products or to reinforce their own history and heritage. Frith promotions have been used by Hovis bread, Courage beers, Scots Porage Oats, Colman's mustard, Cadbury's foods, Mellow Birds coffee, Dunhill pipe tobacco, Guinness, and Bulmer's Cider.

Genealogy and Family History

As the interest in family history and roots grows world-wide, more and more people are turning to Frith's photographs of Great Britain for images of the towns, villages and streets where their ancestors lived; and, of course, photographs of the churches and chapels where their ancestors were christened, married and buried are an essential part of every genealogy tree and family album.

Frith Products

All Frith photographs are available Framed or just as Mounted Prints and Posters (size 23 x 16 inches). These may be ordered from the address below. From time to time other products - Address Books, Calendars, Table Mats, etc - are available.

The Internet

Already twenty thousand Frith photographs can be viewed and purchased on the internet through the Frith websites and a myriad of partner sites.

For more detailed information on Frith companies and products, look at these sites:

www.francisfrith.co.uk
www.francisfrith.com
(for North American visitors)

See the complete list of Frith Books at:
www.francisfrith.co.uk
This web site is regularly updated with the latest list of publications from the Frith Book Company. If you wish to buy books relating to another part of the country that your local bookshop does not stock, you may purchase on-line.

For further information, trade, or author enquiries please contact us at the address below:
The Francis Frith Collection, Frith's Barn, Teffont, Salisbury, Wiltshire, England SP3 5QP.
Tel: +44 (0)1722 716 376 Fax: +44 (0)1722 716 881   Email: sales@francisfrith.co.uk

See Frith books on the internet www.francisfrith.co.uk

To receive your **FREE** Mounted Print

Mounted Print
Overall size 14 x 11 inches

Cut out this Voucher and return it with your remittance for £1.95 to cover postage and handling, to UK addresses. For overseas addresses please include £4.00 post and handling. Choose any photograph included in this book. Your SEPIA print will be A4 in size, and mounted in a cream mount with burgundy rule line, overall size 14 x 11 inches.

Order additional Mounted Prints at HALF PRICE (only £7.49 each*)

If there are further pictures you would like to order, possibly as gifts for friends and family, purchase them at half price (no additional postage and handling required).

Have your Mounted Prints framed*

For an additional £14.95 per print you can have your chosen Mounted Print framed in an elegant polished wood and gilt moulding, overall size 16 x 13 inches (no additional postage and handling required).

---

* IMPORTANT!
These special prices are only available if ordered using the original voucher on this page (no copies permitted) and at the same time as your free Mounted Print, for delivery to the same address

---

Frith Collectors' Guild

From time to time we publish a magazine of news and stories about Frith photographs and further special offers of Frith products. If you would like 12 months FREE membership, please return this form.

Send completed forms to:
The Francis Frith Collection, Frith's Barn, Teffont, Salisbury, Wiltshire SP3 5QP

Voucher for **FREE** and Reduced Price Frith Prints

Picture no.	Page number	Qty	Mounted @ £7.49	Framed + £14.95	Total Cost
		1	**Free of charge***	£	£
			£7.49	£	£
			£7.49	£	£
			£7.49	£	£
			£7.49	£	£
			£7.49	£	£

Please allow 28 days for delivery   *** Post & handling**   **£1.95**

Book Title . . . .   **Total Order Cost**   **£**

Please do not photocopy this voucher. Only the original is valid, so please cut it out and return it to us.

I enclose a cheque / postal order for £ . . . .
made payable to 'The Francis Frith Collection'
OR please debit my Mastercard / Visa / Switch / Amex card
(credit cards please on all overseas orders)

Number . . . .

Issue No(Switch only) . . . . .Valid from (Amex/Switch) . . . .

Expires . . . .   Signature . . . .

Name Mr/Mrs/Ms . . . .

Address . . . .

. . . .

. . . . Postcode . . . .

Daytime Tel No . . . .   **VALID TO 31/12/05**

The Francis Frith Collectors' Guild

Please enrol me as a member for 12 months free of charge.

Name Mr/Mrs/Ms . . . .

Address . . . .

. . . .

. . . . Postcode . . . .

Would you like to find out more about Francis Frith?

We have recently recruited some entertaining speakers who are happy to visit local groups, clubs and societies to give an illustrated talk documenting Frith's travels and photographs. If you are a member of such a group and are interested in hosting a presentation, we would love to hear from you.

Our speakers bring with them a small selection of our local town and county books, together with sample prints. They are happy to take orders. A small proportion of the order value is donated to the group who have hosted the presentation. The talks are therefore an excellent way of fundraising for small groups and societies.

Can you help us with information about any of the Frith photographs in this book?

We are gradually compiling an historical record for each of the photographs in the Frith archive. It is always fascinating to find out the names of the people shown in the pictures, as well as insights into the shops, buildings and other features depicted.

If you recognize anyone in the photographs in this book, or if you have information not already included in the author's caption, do let us know. We would love to hear from you, and will try to publish it in future books or articles.

Our production team

Frith books are produced by a small dedicated team at offices in the converted Grade II listed 18th-century barn at Teffont near Salisbury, illustrated above. Most have worked with the Frith Collection for many years. All have in common one quality: they have a passion for the Frith Collection. The team is constantly expanding, but currently includes:

Jason Buck, John Buck, Douglas Burns, Heather Crisp, Lucy Elcock, Isobel Hall, Rob Hames, Hazel Heaton, Peter Horne, James Kinnear, Tina Leary, Hannah Marsh, Eliza Sackett, Terence Sackett, Sandra Sanger, Lewis Taylor, Shelley Tolcher, Helen Vimpany, Clive Wathen and Jenny Wathen.